SUPER SIMPLE

HALLOWEEN

ACTIVITIES

FUN AND EASY HOLIDAY PROJECTS FOR KIDS

Megan Borgert-Spaniol

Consulting Editor, Diane Craig, M.A./Reading Specialist

Super Sandcastle

An Imprint of Abdo Publishing
abdopublishing.com

abdopublishing.com

Published by Abdo Publishing, a division of ABDO, PO Box 398166, Minneapolis, Minnesota 55439.
Copyright © 2018 by Abdo Consulting Group, Inc. International copyrights reserved in all countries.
No part of this book may be reproduced in any form without written permission from the publisher.
Super SandCastle™ is a trademark and logo of Abdo Publishing.

Printed in the United States of America, North Mankato, Minnesota

102017
012018

THIS BOOK CONTAINS
RECYCLED MATERIALS

Design: Alison Stuerman, Mighty Media, Inc.
Production: Mighty Media, Inc.
Editor: Rebecca Felix
Cover Photographs: Mighty Media, Inc.; Shutterstock
Interior Photographs: iStockphoto; Mighty Media, Inc.; Shutterstock

The following manufacturers/names appearing in this book are trademarks:
Craft Smart®, Elmer's®, Fiskars®, Marvy® Uchida Chalk Marker, Mod Podge®, Scotch®, Sharpie®

Publisher's Cataloging-in-Publication Data

Names: Borgert-Spaniol, Megan, author.
Title: Super simple Halloween activities: fun and easy holiday projects for kids /
by Megan Borgert-Spaniol.
Other titles: Fun and easy holiday projects for kids
Description: Minneapolis, Minnesota : Abdo Publishing, 2018. | Series: Super simple holidays |
Identifiers: LCCN 2017946525 | ISBN 9781532112454 (lib.bdg.) | ISBN 9781614799870 (ebook)
Subjects: LCSH: Halloween decorations--Juvenile literature. | Handicraft--Juvenile literature. |
    Holiday decorations--Juvenile literature.
Classification: DDC 745.59416--dc23
LC record available at https://lccn.loc.gov/2017946525

Super SandCastle™ books are created by a team of professional educators, reading specialists,
and content developers around five essential components—phonemic awareness, phonics,
vocabulary, text comprehension, and fluency—to assist young readers as they develop reading
skills and strategies and increase their general knowledge. All books are written, reviewed,
and leveled for guided reading and early reading intervention for use in shared, guided, and
independent reading and writing activities to support a balanced approach to literacy instruction.

TO ADULT HELPERS

The craft projects in this series are fun and simple. There are just a few things to remember to keep kids safe. Some projects involve the use of food items with allergy triggers. Also, kids may be using messy materials such as glue or paint. Make sure they protect their clothes and work surfaces. Review the projects before starting and be ready to assist when necessary.

KEY SYMBOL

Watch for this warning symbol in this book. Here is what it means.

NUTS!

This project includes the use of nuts. Find out whether anyone you are serving has a nut allergy.

CONTENTS

HAPPY HOLIDAYS!

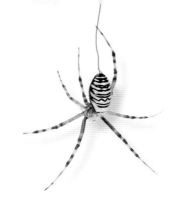

Holidays are great times to celebrate with family and friends. Many people have favorite holiday **traditions**. Some traditions are hundreds of years old. But people start new traditions too, such as making holiday foods and crafts.

HALLOWEEN

Some Halloween **traditions** date back to an ancient yearly celebration called Samhain. People believed ghosts returned to Earth during Samhain. Some people lit candles to guide the ghosts.

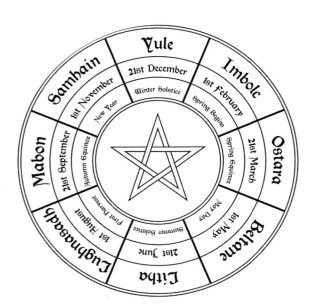

When **Christianity** formed, All Saints' Day took place on November 1. The first full day of Samhain is celebrated on this day too. The day before, October 31, became known as All Hallows' Eve. Later, it was called Halloween.

CELEBRATE HALLOWEEN

Halloween has several common **traditions** throughout many countries. Do you celebrate using any of these traditions?

COSTUMES

During Samhain, people often wore masks or animal skins. They did this so the ghosts would not recognize them. Later, people dressed as saints, angels, and **devils**. Today, people dress up as many different characters on Halloween.

TRICK-OR-TREAT

Hundreds of years ago, people in Ireland and Scotland wore costumes to visit other homes. They sang songs or told jokes at each door in exchange for food or coins. Today, children in costumes visit other homes on Halloween. They ask for treats at each door.

PUMPKIN CARVING

Long ago, people in Ireland and Great Britain carved faces into **root vegetables** at Halloween. This **tradition** spread to North America. There, people carved faces into pumpkins to celebrate the holiday.

MATERIALS

Here are some of the materials that you will need for the projects in this book.

CARD STOCK

CARDBOARD

CARDBOARD
EGG CARTON

CLEAR GLASS JAR

CRAFT GLUE

FLAT ROCKS WITH
ONE STRAIGHT
EDGE

GAUZE

GOOGLY EYES

MARKERS

MINI DONUTS

MOD PODGE
MATTE

NEWSPAPER

PAINT

PAINTBRUSHES

PAPER TOWEL
TUBE

PEANUT BUTTER

PLASTIC SPIDERS

PRETZELS

REESE'S PIECES
CANDIES

RIBBON

SCISSORS

SMALL HEAVY
BALL

SOUP CAN

STRING

TAPE

TOOTHPICKS

WHITE CHALK
MARKER

WOODEN CRAFT
STICKS

WOODEN SKEWERS

YARN

GHOST GREETING CARD

Send someone a spooky surprise with this pop-up card!

WHAT YOU NEED

black & white card stock

scissors

black marker

tape

white chalk marker

googly eyes or spooky stickers

craft glue

1 Fold a black piece of card stock in half. **Crease** the edge.

2 Fold a white piece of card stock in half. Crease the edge.

3 Place the scissors on the creased fold of the white card stock, and closer to either the top or bottom edge. Cut at an angle toward the opposite edge of the card.

4 Open the larger piece of white card stock. The point will be the bottom of the ghost. Cut the two sides and the top of the card stock into a ghost shape.

(continued on next page)

5 Use the black marker to draw the ghost's eyes and mouth.

6 Fold the ghost on the **crease**. Make sure the ghost's mouth and eyes are facing out.

7 Open the black card stock so the crease is on the left. Set the folded ghost upside down inside the card. Place it so the bottom of the ghost's crease touches the card's fold line.

8 Unfold the ghost, keeping it in place. Tape one side of the bottom edge to one half of the card.

TIP Add a second, mini ghost to your card! Just repeat steps 3 and 4, making a smaller ghost.

9 Tape the other side of the ghost's bottom edge to the other half of the card.

10 Close the card and press where the tape is.

11 Open the card. The ghost should pop up!

12 Write "BOO!" inside the card in white chalk marker.

13 Decorate the outside of the card using googly eyes or spooky stickers. Then give it to someone you want to surprise!

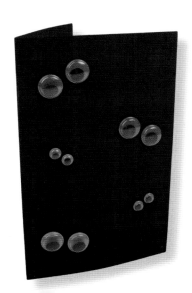

CANDY CORN GARLAND

Create a cool strand of classic Halloween sweets!

WHAT YOU NEED

scissors

cardboard

marker

pencil

white, yellow & orange card stock

craft glue

ribbon

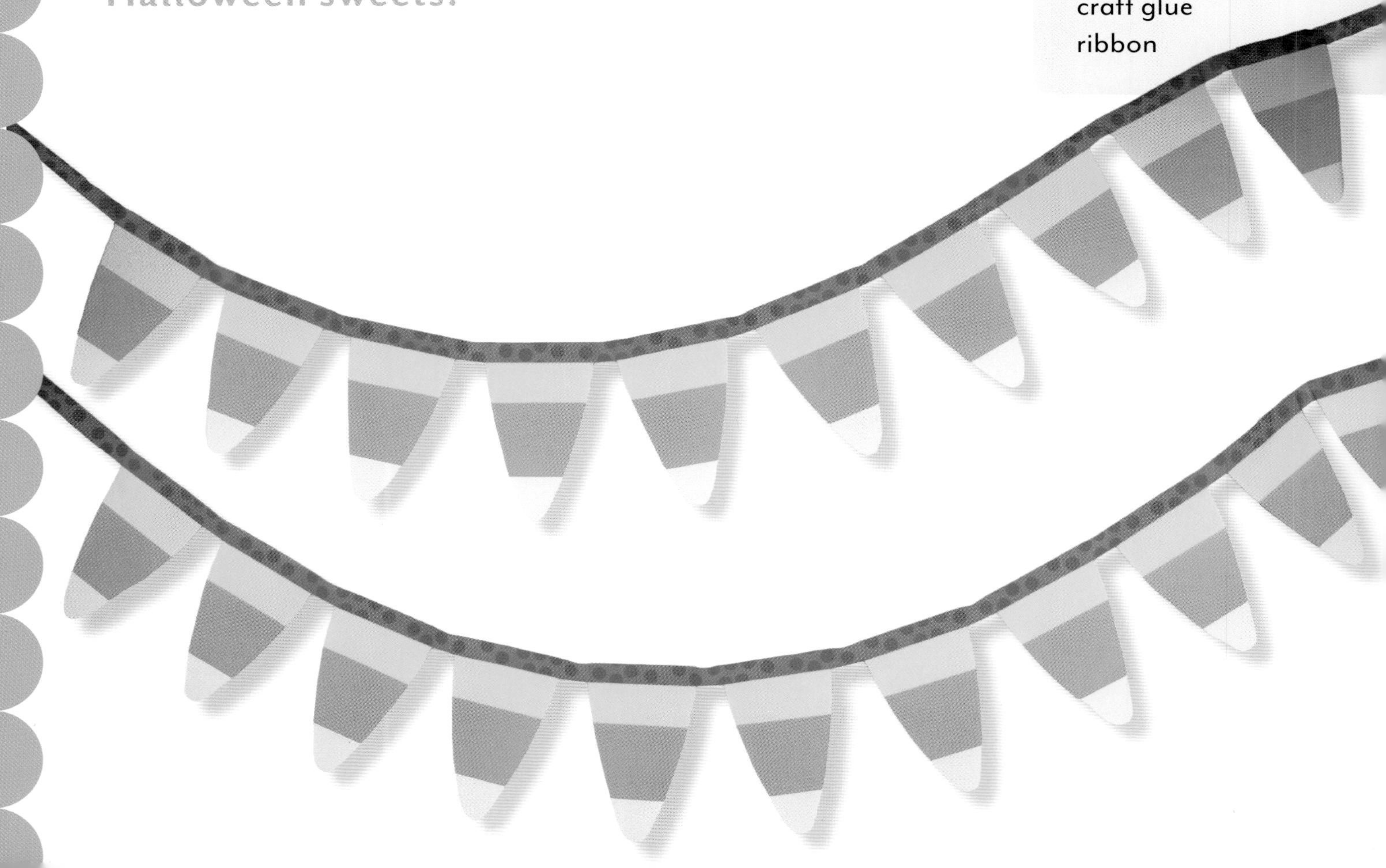

1 Cut a candy corn shape out of cardboard. Trace it on the cardboard and cut out the shape. Write "WHITE" on one shape.

2 Cut the unlabeled shape in thirds. Write "YELLOW" on the widest third. Write "ORANGE" on the middle third. Recycle the final third. The three labeled shapes are **templates**.

3 Trace the templates on the white, yellow, and orange card stock. Cut out the shapes.

4 Glue a yellow piece over the wide end of a white piece. Glue an orange piece so its top edge **overlaps** the bottom of the yellow piece. Line up all side edges.

5 Repeat steps 3 and 4 to make more candy corns.

6 Cut a long piece of ribbon. Glue it to the wide end of each candy corn. Let the glue dry. Then hang your candy **garland**!

SWEET SPIDERS

These spindly spiders are scrumptious, not scary!

WHAT YOU NEED

pretzels
mini donuts
dinner knife
peanut butter
Reese's Pieces candies

1 Break the pretzels to create curved pieces for the legs. Make eight pieces for each spider you want to create.

2 Stick eight pretzel pieces into a mini donut to look like spider legs.

3 Spread a bit of peanut butter on one side of a Reese's Pieces candy. Stick the candy to the mini donut to make an eye. Repeat with another piece of candy and more peanut butter to make a second eye.

4 Repeat steps 1 through 3 to make more spiders. Then share your sweet snacks with family and friends!

GHOST BOWLING

Send ghouls flying with a round of ghost bowling!

WHAT YOU NEED

black felt

scissors

double-sided tape

10 rolls of toilet paper

masking tape

measuring tape

small heavy ball

1 Cut ten large ovals out of the black felt. These will be the ghosts' mouths.

2 Cut 20 small ovals out of the felt. These will be the ghosts' eyes.

3 Use double-sided tape to attach the eyes and mouths onto the toilet paper rolls.

4 Arrange the toilet paper rolls in a **pyramid** on the floor.

5 Place a line of masking tape on the floor 10 feet (3 m) from the pyramid. This is where players will stand to bowl.

6 Take turns rolling the ball toward the pyramid. See who can knock down the most ghosts!

TIP Make creative ghost faces! Cut different shapes for the eyes and mouths.

STRINGY SPIDERWEBS

Weave colorful webs to create a creepy Halloween mood!

WHAT YOU NEED

newspaper

wooden craft sticks

paint

paintbrush

craft glue

scissors

measuring tape

black &
   orange yarn

plastic spiders

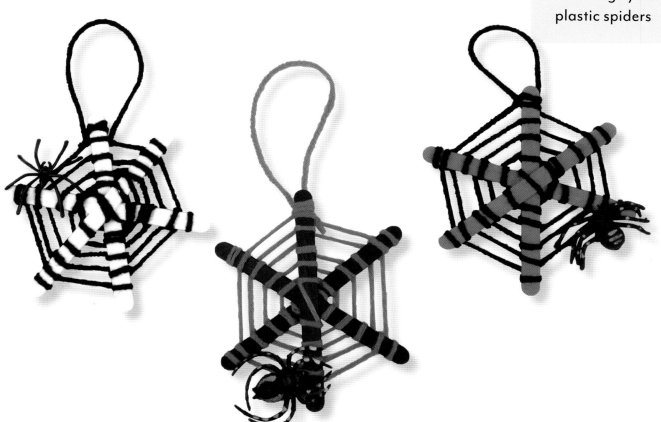

20

1 Cover your work surface with newspaper. Paint three craft sticks for each web you want to make. Let the paint dry.

2 Glue three craft sticks together as shown. Let the glue dry.

3 Cut a 7-foot (2 m) piece of yarn. Tie one end around the middle of the craft sticks.

4 Wrap the yarn around a craft stick. Then wrap it around the next craft stick. Continue wrapping the yarn around the sticks until the web is complete.

5 Tie the yarn to the last craft stick. Cut the yarn 6 inches (15 cm) from the knot. Tie the end of the yarn around the same stick to make a loop.

6 Glue a plastic spider to the web. Let the glue dry.

7 Repeat steps 2 through 6 to make more webs. Then hang them for the holiday!

21

FRANK-CAN-STEIN'S MONSTER

Give an old can new life as a green Frankenstein's monster!

WHAT YOU NEED

newspaper

empty soup or coffee can

green paint

foam paintbrush

black felt

ruler

scissors

strong adhesive

googly eyes

button

black marker

2 nuts

2 bolts

1 Cover your work surface with newspaper. Paint the can green. Let the paint dry.

2 Cut the felt into a circle. Make the circle's **diameter** at least 2 inches (5 cm) larger than the diameter of the can.

3 Cut small triangles around the edge of the circle to make it look **ragged**. This is the monster's hair.

4 Glue the hair onto the closed end of the can. Fold its ragged edges over the edge of the can and glue them down.

5 Glue googly eyes and a button nose to the can. Draw a mouth and some **scars**.

6 Screw the nuts onto the ends of the bolts. Glue one combination to each side of the can. Let the glue dry.

7 Set your Frankenstein's monster anywhere you want to give someone a fright!

23

GLOWING MUMMY

Make a mummy to haunt the dark corners of your home!

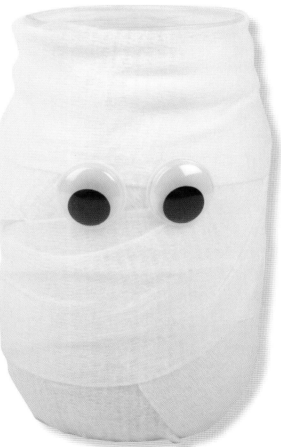

WHAT YOU NEED
newspaper
clear glass jar
Mod Podge Matte
foam brush
roll of gauze
craft glue
googly eyes
small
battery-operated
candle

24

1 Cover your work surface with newspaper. Coat the outside of the jar with Mod Podge Matte.

2 Wrap gauze around the jar several times. Let the layers of gauze **overlap** in different directions.

3 Glue googly eyes to the gauze. This completes the mummy's face. Mummy mouths and noses are often covered up! Let the glue dry.

4 Turn on the small battery-operated candle. Place it in the jar. Watch your mummy come to life with a soft glow!

BAT MOBILE

These bats flutter and fly, but won't bite!

WHAT YOU NEED

- cardboard egg carton
- scissors
- marker
- wooden skewer
- newspaper
- black paint
- paintbrush
- googly eyes
- craft glue
- paper towel tube
- pencil
- string
- tape
- toothpick

1 Cut a row of three cups from an egg carton. Cut off the extra carton around the edges.

2 Draw two arches on the front and back sides of the end cups.

3 Cut out the arches. This makes the bat's wings.

4 Repeat steps 1 through 3 to make two more bats.

5 Use a wooden skewer to poke a hole in the top of the middle section of each bat.

6 Cover your work surface with newspaper. Paint the bats black. Let the paint dry.

7 Glue a set of googly eyes on each bat. Let the glue dry.

(continued on next page)

8 Push the skewer through the paper towel tube to make a set of holes. Make one set of holes for each bat. Space the sets evenly apart.

9 Paint the tube black. Let it dry.

10 Cut a long piece of string. Run it through the ends of the tube. Tie the ends in a knot. This makes a triangle you will use to hang the **mobile**.

11 Cut another long piece of string. Tape it to a toothpick. Thread the toothpick and string through one set of holes on the paper towel tube.

12 Run the toothpick and thread through the hole in the top of one bat.

13 Remove the toothpick. Tie the end of the string several times to make a large knot. This keeps the string from slipping through the hole once the bat is hanging.

14 Repeat steps 11 through 13 to hang the other bats.

15 Hang the bats at different lengths. To hang a bat at a shorter length, pull up on its string so the bat hangs closer to the paper towel tube. Knot the string above the tube. Trim the **excess** string.

16 Hang your holiday **mobile** and watch the bats take flight!

29

SPOOKY STONE CEMETERY

Build your own bone-chilling mini graveyard!

WHAT YOU NEED

newspaper

green, brown, & gray paint

paintbrush

paper plate

flat rocks with one straight edge

black paint pen

clay

moss

craft glue

artificial cobwebs

1 Cover your work surface with newspaper. Paint the plate green. Add some brown paint to look like dirt. Let the paint dry.

2 Paint the rocks gray. Let the paint dry.

3 Place a rock with the flat edge facing you. Write "RIP" in paint pen. This stands for "rest in peace." Come up with other **gravestone** messages and write them on the other rocks.

4 Use clay to stick the straight edge of each rock on the plate.

5 Glue bits of moss to the plate.

6 Stretch out cobwebs and lay them over the moss to look like fog.

7 Set out your **cemetery** as a spooky Halloween decoration!

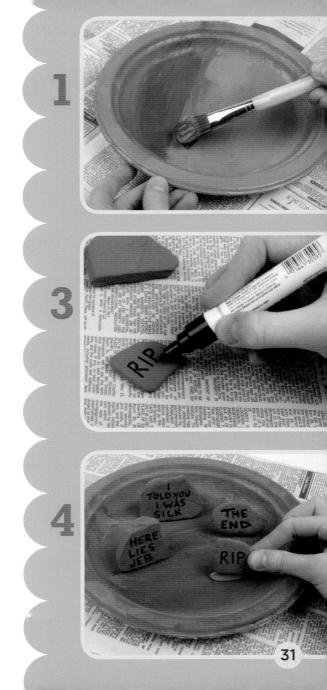

GLOSSARY

cemetery – a place where dead people or pets are buried.

Christianity – a religion that follows the teachings of Jesus Christ.

crease – to make a sharp line in something by folding it. This line is also called a crease.

devil – the spirit of evil in many religions, or a wicked person or being.

diameter – the distance across the middle of a circle.

garland – a decorative ring or rope made of leaves, flowers, or some other material.

loop – a circle made by a rope, string, or thread.

mobile – an artistic device with parts that are arranged so they will move in the air currents.

overlap – to lie partly on top of something.

pyramid – a three-dimensional shape with triangular sides that form a point at the top.

ragged – having an irregular edge or outline.

root vegetable – a vegetable that grows under the ground. Potatoes and carrots are root vegetables.

scar – a mark left on the skin after a cut heals.

template – a shape or pattern that is drawn or cut around to make the same shape in another material.

tradition – a belief or practice passed through a family or group of people.